New Age Poetry

John Flanagan

chipmunkapublishing
the mental health publisher

John Flanagan

Published by
Chipmunkapublishing
PO Box 6872
Brentwood
Essex CM13 1ZT
United Kingdom

http://www.chipmunkapublishing.com

Edited by Drucilla Impleton

Chipmunkapublishing gratefully acknowledge the support of Arts Council England.

The Magic of Mermaids

Mermaids live in coral castles under the sea
Far off from the ignorant mere mortal man
Mermaids are magic they communicate by
telepathy
And know all secrets of a healthy life span
Mermaids ride dolphins like they were sea horses
That outlandish ocean sport we must not ban.

Miranda the mermaid was so humanly disguised
The Scarborough council she met were hypnotised
Her idea was it not fun an original one
Build a sea wave sculpture on the North Bay
Build it not of traditional concrete and clay
But of material that ripples on a breezy day.

The magic of mermaids is a deep mystery
How they guide the albatross in its flight
Over our sparkling blue ocean is beyond me
Enchanting enticing mermaids swim a silent sea
Skins as a pale ivory and head hair like kelp
Scaley fishtails slap living waters constantly

No disaster hero no mariner cried for help

Who knew this was a myth but what if.

New Age Poetry

Friends on Earth

If you see me fretful or forlorn you oppose it so

Inspiring sunny infectious joy spaced way within me

If you hear my trembling voice you by now know

Desire is like a rare wine for us to share

If I smell your flowery female summer ripe perfume

My clock like heart beats a quickening rhythm

Compared only with an ever echoed cannon ball

boom

If I taste your sweet warm honey flavoured lips

My senses are touched by love born beyond the

womb.

Friends on earth are proud as rooted forest trees

As rivers flow high and low merging at the seas

As magnificent mountains were there when time

was young

As ageing history we know repeats itself

dramatically

The story of our lives develop like a song never

unsung

As the ocean's oysters are abundant few shelter a
pearl

Friends on earth tell the truth dampening the devil's
tongue

As elemental storms wreck havoc under skies
cursed by thunder

As sunlight soothes our spirits again no time for
fear

Friends on earth love life and always stay sincere.

No News is Good News

What a desperate and sick world we all live in
Will anyone ever lose this war with money or win
Were rogue butchers treating meat with deadly
bacteria
Unaware we try stay healthy eating tainted food
How many people must fall ill suffering from
wisteria
Count up those innocents infected by Satan's
brood.

Money the root of all evil temps mankind who kills
In vain any junkie will obtain drugs for sexual thrills
In pain any junkie get's the needle time and time
again
Insane are they who allow their bodies to wilt and
wane.

Money the source of all evil encourages mankind
who kills
How are oilrig owners keen on safety when oil spills

Why should our coastlines be contaminated and
wildlife die
Is it a collective effort this worldwide global warming
Why are the seas rising and awesome hurricanes
storming
We fear earthquakes ever active and volcanoes
never extinct.

Unscrupulous big game hunters kill animals for
sport
Must man be saved from beast or beast from man
If we spoilers are clever how do we get caught
If all government's are wise impose a world ban.

New Age Poetry

Yesteryears

There was a time I feel compelled to tell
When we threw coins down the wishing well
Heaven you implicitly believed in but not so hell
If greeted by some stranger you volunteered to smile
In our yesteryears we were individual with style.

How I grazed both knees climbing hills climbing trees
Stampeding through stinging nettles you solved those problems
By boat I sailed canals inhaled the scented breeze
My body this mobile mystic temple sacred and strong
I confessed to loving life if that is wrong.

Ruth was the wild child who flowered from youth
The cat that did scare the manlike mouse
She was rebellious by nature to tell the truth
She designed every fantasy room at her house.

Her character zodiac sign proved compatible with
mine.
Living in bygone times was simple not sophisticated
The terrors of technology were as then underrated
And marriage we honoured more so than divorce
In yesteryears money was no real remedy for
remorse.

New Age Poetry

Adult Adolescence

Act your age but not your shoe size
I told the truth you told me sympathetic lies
Of education you were wary it was scary
In a maze no doubt no obvious pathway out
So now you need this emotive epic rescue.

It was like pistols at dawn a drama duel
Son challenged father with water gun fuel
Your attempts at kinship were more than less
remote
You are old yet young how do you cope
There is help for you there is hope.

Live and learn or we will not live long
Yes you swore at me that I was wrong
How I realised it was a massive heartache
Why is it now that my poor nerves quake
So near to me your temper tantrums I fear
No respect will kill our love be sincere.

His devoted mother always at his beckon call

She nurtured him when he was baby small
What of to day his ill behaviour beguiles us all.

Images from a Decade

Hungry for wealth for power the farmer rapes the
fertile lands
Every minute every hour we are expanding those
desert sands
The freezing iceberg artic regions are melting who
understands
Or tropical rain forests are drying up is man's
pleasure now his pain
When the animals we did cherish get hunted down
for material gain.

Perverted priests do frolic with drugged children
under a moonlight night
Around a coven campfire all swore satin is their
guiding light
But when daytime dawned those cowled witches
did take to flight.

The prostitute open for business flaunts her seedy
trade

She services the general public from frustrations
first grade
Decency was cast away for her lusty body you
blindly paid
Law and order is not what it was criminals laugh
and scorn
To see some forlorn police force practice soft porn.

Caravan gypsies are raggedly rich and right on
their own
They live off this land sucking meat from the bone
They will tell you your fortune is not as great as
theirs
When you walked quickly from a hundred carnival
fairs.

Money is a resourceful river with a currency flow
We get everywhere with it without it nowhere for
sure
Brave a glance at them beggars out on the stony
city street
All seem so destitute so hopelessly incomplete

New Age Poetry

But which of those in disguise treks back to a
homely retreat.

Probing deep carpeted oceans and mountains
towering into the sky
Man must risk his life for fame its do or die
We ask ourselves in a lonely windblown moment
why
Beyond our earthly atmosphere is an ever-present
fear
Should those industrial gases continue damaging
the ozone layer.

Our snaking rivers our diamond seas were once
mirror clear
Then those chemical merchants did decide that
they should interfere
Polluting the fishy waterways crediting damage to
the taxpayer.

The First Spring Miracle

Gone by the hazardous winter spell, which stunned
us as can a bell
Upon us is the birth of blissful spring its symphonic
secrets to sell.

In that single month of early May white petalled
daisies do gently jingle
In response to a cool light breeze, which can just
stimulate our imagination
Silver scaled salmon fly up the frothy waterfall their
natural cycle to complete
Where heather shrubs are scattered on smooth
grass hills in gay constellation
Silver birch trees are featured there basking from a
naked sun's holy heat
Where soft rain pellets descend on wide emerald
green meadows a shepherd
Is returning to his beloved mountain ushering
before him one score of goats
Upon wrinkled pathways his sandaled feet disrupt
loose stones then time stirred

And olive green frogs were heard croaking on the
cream lilied water pond.

Masses of fleecy white clouds sail majestically in
bright blue southern skies
Below fragrant gases ooze out from the hollow
ravine here animals are seen
The red fox prowls through woodlands exhibiting its
crafty face of scowls
Hundreds of oval leaves litter the knife-edged turf
tinged with beryl green
And in a flash one furry badger burrows its way out
from dense thick underbrush
And hesitates at questioning our perfumed air that
now excites his whole being
A slender bodied weasel shakes her whiskers for
she chases mice, which rush.
Dragonflies traverse the tingling morning air beating
their net – veined wings
Warm sunny rays skitter over a broad mumbling
creek's cool crystal surface.

From dead wood slate grey smoke plumes curl

higher above this crazy yellow fire

A small elfin figure is seated near to tall tawny rock

boulders drawing power

One spell herself did select fell on the wren its

throat sang never yet to tire

Dramatically the strangely garbed dwarf put down

his blunt hammer and sharp pick

And quick leg strides took him verily into that

presence where mistress magic

Dressed in cherry red cotton garments stroked her

willow wand a star trick

Drew his tender senses away from abstract

symbols now he groped for future tenses

By which to explain himself when she vanished he

stood on a bedrock shelf

Raptly gazing over at featherlike green ferns

growing wild by clotted tree land.

Vanilla and coffee haired mermaids take rest upon

rugged salty sea wet rocks

They with all fingers alerted mellowly play

whalebone harps an act concerted

New Age Poetry

Armour plated marine horses swarm beneath coral

reefs lulled by music free

On the tide washed beach trimmed with shingle

little crabs thread crooked paths

Between bleached white pepples where laces of

liquid water graces sand there

The jagged earth stone gorge glints reflections from

an egg yoke yellow sun.

Up from this silver shoreline are honeysuckle

bushes a pride to the noon forest

Up then diving to ground the thrush creates havoc

cracking snails against a rock

Scented pine trees keep forcing their growth their

needle like leaves are blest.

The First Autumn Miracle

Good summer rolled away as autumn came its
season treasures copper and gold
The first autumn is revealed as an old October sun
erratically wheeled
In a blue Tuesday sky pearl white clouds shift over
this gay harlequin land
On earth dark brown tanned shadows tremble
besides trees smeared in rain water
One wide bed of grass tinted cabbage green
gleamed like new emeralds upon sand
Amber sunlight ripples across a swift stream to
where hard rocky banks lie
Fish in yellow flocks fly beneath the farmer who
ripens all crops to die.

Costumed in strawberry blonde hair a dog danced
on the gravel road to nowhere
Lost winds gently gurgle and twist inside this rusty
leaf coated forest
Silver stallions are exposed grazing around velvet
pastures spun with fences

New Age Poetry

Dandelions like an epidemic are spread about they
put scientists to the test
Schools of sparrow's wing like feathered bullets
they surprise our senses
Within the haunted forests heart rainbow insects
swim the sifting air
Grey uniformed squirrels parade about collecting
nuts and baked berries to store
Against that refrigerated winter which spells certain
death but no more
The tidal winds growl again sending one million
unemployed leafs to the floor
Where pools of umbrella toadstools grow splashed
by warm sunlit shadows

Two thousand trumpet daffodils punctuate the
damp air with weird tunes
Which tell of the tortured human slaves locked in
deep in hollow dry caves
How they prayed for freedom's wine seemingly
bottled away forever in civil runes
The sly thin legged October spider spins its elastic
web with tragedy as glue

The forked tail swallow dives between sleeping
trees and sparkling green hills
Quick as a moment it went leaving only shivering
patterns to see through.

Clusters of clover decorate a ribboned road upon
this one traveller strolls
But his eyes held heaven bred grace from which
every poor soul is fed
But his clothes were wilted as in each torn pocket
time had made large holes
People like lost phantoms drifted around a pale
blue mirrored lake
Before him pale chestnut mountains spiralled way
up into blankets of cloud
Before him was this ever productive sea cursing his
mind with gems to take
But alas man has captured its law its throbbing
music raw and often loud.

Bonfires are burning our lonely sorrow that linked
us from a passed tomorrow

New Age Poetry

That major event which first enticed me is spent
with no time to borrow.
Now the scorched earth listens as circus children
roam its sunken valleys
Children cross wood carved bridges and disturb the
spiced dust of empty years
Now the sighing earth opens its pores and
everywhere is infected by mist
Swirling aimless like tasteless tobacco smoke it
sparks off man's hidden fears
Suddenly the alien haze melted as turbulent sun
fired its yellow rays always.

The First Summer Miracle

The earth's temperature slowly boils as lady
summer becomes actively aware
From a lake of grass she rose to tread her bed
ablaze with wild flowers
At once magnetic august figure lilac orchids adorn
her golden hair
Her voice like sweet wine whisperingly told you the
good and evil powers
Skylark birds flocked gladly chirping their chorus of
love no time to spare.

Sunlight focused itself through an azure ocean blue
bleached sky
Impregnated with floating islands of creamy candy
floss morning clouds
Where giant terracotta elm trees were thatched in
blazing emerald leafs
The ground soil far around was cracked baked hot
like a cake from an oven
Tortoiseshell with cabbage white butterflies on air
weave a flittering dance

New Age Poetry

Drugged from the dusty heat of that billion year
volcanic like eternal sun
But feel it a minted baby breeze tenderly touches
down upon all life anyway
Murmuring yet soundless over ripe corn and barley
fields in time to sell
Or over semi-parched enchanted praires where
wandering gipsy warriors dwell
One silver flecked stream trembles over green
weed clogged rocks
On a current journey to the deeply mysterious
mother sea no doubt
Here at some deserted lagoon glittering coral caves
are revealed as the relentless tide ebbs out.

Somewhere under this vivid blue velvet sky brown
tanned lady summer starts
Creating an affair for our rose scented day so busy
as buzzing bees
She quickens but never sickens the ever hungry
native hearts
Or the bodies of impassioned lovers old and young
as they together wrestle

Like a beast she's all passion always altering the
common vogue
Her favourite pet is the boldest yet formed of a lion
with eagles wings
A graceful guardian he is known to be something of
a riotous rogue
He is time moving surely as unlimited desert
mirages glow and shimmer
Like an enormous blanket etched in growing
shapes and smiling tones
Where the humped sandy oasis lays encrusted with
priceless diamond stones
An unknown harlequin drinks pure wine from the
thorned cactus
He has seen the phoenix consumed in fire then rise
renewed again
From its charcoal ashes its immortality teased
humanity with pain
A turbaned man performs an amazing Indian rope
trick
Over red hot coals like a human candle around a
twisted wick

New Age Poetry

As long stemmed trumpet music amplifies

hypnotically through the market place

People slither like lusty snakes for they share that

same face.

Look away on another part of the veined map our

friendly lord summer

Bathes in the mountain creek with any wild beast

he may dare speak

At his wilderness cabin anyone is a welcome guest

there's no endurance test

But sole survival we know from fate is not always

for us the best

So from everyone's face each puzzled doubt or

sour frown he could take

And show to you a sun kissed day upon a turquoise

blue mirrored lake

Painted with white virgin swans which tremble on

the watery surface

Or point at ivy sculptured castles where clever

wizards meet to trick or treat

Or he will tell you when gossamer haired nymphs

dance naked free altogether

 By weeping willow trees by bubbling brooks they
catch their fish to eat
The fish rainbow armoured are as living jewels in
those crinkled waterways.

The First Winter Miracle

Darkness dissolved as a December dawn bathed
our world in music and lights
The blushed eastern sun rose to kiss the silent
sleepy land with its warmth
The new morning skies are dyed azure blue blotted
across with puffy clouds
Thus came nine doves divine all tongues were
shard like a trumpet that blared
Thus came this lone minstrel named love one lyric
to fit us as would a glove
A fairy princess passed through Christmas holly
bushes which could only sigh
A painted gypsy caravan is bracketed by leaf
bronze tress which just multiply
Billions of tiny dust motes fall from their snakelike
branches and forever lie
On stiff corduroy grass dead sepia brown leaves
form a puzzling jigsaw frown.

Cutting the cold air like a knife two magpies let joy
and sorrow lilt into life

Alarmed this glossy blackbird fled away with its
prize one worm of small size
Northern reindeer roam the marshy woodlands
they're hunted so far from home
An armada of red robins raced against time they be
pious keepers of holy rhyme
The gallant court jester shuffles on a rock road his
ruby robes smile in ruffles
From where moody winds grumbling had struck
them then left away weakly rumbling
Herbal plants grew up at distorted angles
suggesting wealth is due is to health
On one murmuring grass ridge was a knotted log
cabin suspended in low gravity
Above white skies just let ricey snow descend no
wild cat felt false lust.

Clothed Christmas children were snow speckled it
shone on one child as fur
Skating around happy valley pond us half folk have
true laughter the common bond
Warm blooded children ride wooden heart welded
sledges down ice feather hills

New Age Poetry

Beyond winter's white veil the universal chapel is
taunted by winds that purr
But inside that holy refuge one huge crowd recited
hymns to get them thrills
Back outside cruel Cold River like an eel wriggled
towards its old mother sea
The gold church bell tolled loud enough to vibrate
souls in heaven or hell
Juniper shrubs with their good berries and scaly
cones are growing just where
An elderly hermit is busy counting every second to
when he will be free.

The mythical dragon sleeps though its right eye
weeps over its lost gem horde
He's imprisoned in eternity mountain the entrance
there of is held by angels
Gold horned opaque white unicorn haunts a forest
glade she's resting from flight
By this star studded road which twists off into that
future January sky
Once more man winter this wizened prophet treads
across a frosty linen plain

His voice sings level and sane as he asks for signs

to see how evil can die

Quivering charcoal shadows in hundreds braid

tapestries around day lit trees

And just above our bright yellow balloon sun casts

swollen sunbeams to earth

And to that rolling old sea water carpet now

streaked in silver and gold.

A Clone Who Me!

If you feel moody staying all alone

Why not risk it skin and bone

Try reproduce yourself as a clone

Who will be you in modern vogue

Swanking off now on the videophone

Think this clone is friend or rogue.

If you see sense use telepathy no pretence

At night or day act contact your clone

At least you are free flirting this identity

It's time your reputation for mischief be known.

My mirrored image is what you are no star

Once you were produced by scientific bacteria

And up grew a new individual but so inferior.

If you feel low staying all alone

Why not risk it skin and bone

Try reproduce yourself as a clone.

Abstract Reality

So sad so far so bad keep your sanity or go mad

Pick up daily news tabloids ask me what we read

Maverick priests preach about sin like it's a fashion

creed

Weighty and hard is this stinging burden we carry

indeed

Look at the way some persecuted adults and

children behave

What wisdom did we use since leaving that

prehistoric cave

Ranting and raving for mammon an idol of gold is

not new

Eat to live not live to eat sticks with us as like glue

Drink to live not live to drink puzzles with no

apparent clue

Who shall save us when the animal lust attacks me

or you.

So rude so crude everybody pains from family

feuds

New Age Poetry

Why fight against an enemy whose face resembles
your own
Why moan and groan those birds from the nest
have flown
Why complain must a summery sun spoil our fragile
attitudes
Why hide from the jewelled rain see what leafy
shrubs do gain
Any family without love is as a ribboned river empty
of fish
Any family no knowledge learning is as a fire
loosing power burning
Any family if they so wish taste success as from a
food dish.

Alien squalling winds howl at scared neglected
council houses
Prejudice stalks this day and night country what
trouble it arouses
Ethnic coloured and white people are restless so ill
at ease
In as stormy time where cruelty copulates with
disease

Red light district prostitute's parade car infested city
streets
Most clients hide their vices or risk a marriage crisis
Drug dealers haunt seedy hotel rooms and
business booms
Drug dealers gamble with human lives rolling
skeleton bone dices
Why these merchants of misery buy train tickets to
hell
Time will tell when fearful they tremble they heard a
holy church bell.

If I were you and you were me how will we interpret
reality
If lady luck blesses our mortal lives with health let it
be
If lady luck beckons us to unknown wealth do follow
or flee.

Adam

Born to us was a beautiful boy a precious gift
Awoken then from innocent babyhood dreams
We were freed from any attention nagging screams
Now he illuminates our happy lives with mirth
And dances to the music of a hot sunny summer
What magic what bliss to see him on earth
Before your eyes he is in cartoon disguise
Outrageous an act this we must not miss.

Fun is what Adam indulges in the best
Tell me he will put anyone to an endurance test
When your sober mood may be somewhat wrong
He will sing out your thoughts like a song.

Back to rambling nature that green therapy cure
As yet Adam our patience he promptly teases
Ever the practical joker jesting how he pleases
Ever the questioner of questions most profound
Ever the scientist who measures the power of
sound.

Advancing with age you see a stressed society
Like never before greedy people steal from the
poor
Adam may you never envy any money mobster
Go travelling your twisting road to far off lands
Go searching for Eve a name to call her
Go find your greatest friend who to you
understands
Love is the basic bread and honey nectar of life
Your personality is flowering from husband and
wife.

Alcoholics Anonymous

She was this party diva great fun with friends

She was a night club dancer a wicked romancer

Smoky laser lights added menace to music trends

Vodka that Stimulant required to enhance her

Inhibitions abandoned for this raunchy singing role

She lost control of abused body and soul

And tasted not the ingredients in her cereal bowl.

He was a high flier a shrewd property buyer

Whiskey like his wife so strong and neat

He was ruthless to us a compulsive liar

Money no problem but life seemed incomplete

He gambled on his family for moral support

One day on a drunken rampage he almost died

Tell me of that allergy or attempted suicide.

We were troubled over the future and the past

Men with women confessing their depressing

stories

We are the alcoholics anonymous and so typecast

Men with women uncertain what the law is

Inspiring me to tell now my birthdates and name

If only you were sober nobody is to blame.

Delusions of Grandeur

Observe how you use your every working day
Tax your imagination on flickering goggle box
screens
Grab that daily tabloid now read what it means
You could exercise hate living in a welfare state
Where people litter streets with 'help me graffiti'
See the abattoir theatre is open would you bring in
a lamb
The dole office doctors are issued luncheon
vouchers
Ain't life hard if we don't weaken our guard.

The rivers are polluted by fish which do not swim
Do you listen at church to Lucifer's hymn
Are you true to love or is your destiny grim
Would we wish for an ideal Singapore dream
No we are busy being anarchists so it may seem
Shall I pick your brain use your ticket for my train
It's a vampire situation a government scheme
creation.

Motoring your precious car on the twisting endless
road
Did your brain squirm out anger and nearly explode
Do you observe like a haloed saint the Highway
Code
Think as petrol smoke spews off its lead poison
From your car up over the hard city road.

The cost of living is ever constantly rising
Pandora's Box I shall not be here advertising
Rich Vultures pluck skin from meek people as they
corrode
Shame on them heathens now it's the end of my
ode.

Fantasy Forest

Follow me down behind grey stone castle walls
Follow the narrow sandy pebbled woodland
footpath
Where over rocky cliffs smoky white water falls
The river runs wild and diverts to a lake
Snow white swans sail on sunny silver waters
They are like proud ships and no mistake
Speckled brown ducks all quacking the flock stirs.

Oak trees and ash and yew trees too
Dominate over miniature valleys sparkling with dew
Honey bees are humming an oriental summer tune
Wild orchids tickled by a breeze gently swoon
Bright cloudy blue skies and nervy painted
butterflies
This clicking magpie bird never whistled any
surprise
Legendary elves are all in time for fantastic fun
Playing on the webbed trampoline that spiders
once spun.

Coned conifers and giant ferns all flourish here

Camouflaged as rock a rabbit was quick to

disappear

No lie we chose freedom my good lady and I

So what if we calmly switched off technology

Mother Nature to me revealed her fruity fantasy.

Focus On Freedom At Filey

Sunlight sparkles on the August summer sea

And watery waves kiss the northern beach at Filey

What a joke seagulls were laughing over us folk

A boy flies his urchin kite against heavenly skies

Happy children skim the air with a starfish Frisbee

Curious children dig this beach for treasure for

trash

Hoping to profit if a gift shop offers cash

Sandy sculptures what commercial art pretty smart

Oh! We were so fearless on that pony ride

And perched there up straight with gleeful pride.

The nautical lifeguard is vigilant is alert to distress

Trying to protect you from danger from

unhappiness

Go canoe or surf the green blue majestic sea

Where boats and yachts sail glittering waters

Or be on shore treat yourself eat seafood

We paid that price it was nice a festive interlude.

John Flanagan

Grannies race electronic wheelchairs over

rendezvous gardens

Here we investigate pleasure and in family tradition

pose

Captured on film by the clicking cameras lens

Fun time for you and me I guess god knows.

Frantic Friday

So here we are itching twitching with apprehension
Wildly excited we aim to relieve pent up tension
Your robot routine damn it know what I mean
Invited are we to a strange house party perhaps
Refuse the pleasure trips they be booby traps
Road rage infects any age and your patience snaps
The rush hour is here you fear its forever.

Time dissolves day to what we recognise as night
Silver stars shimmer through our inky blue sky
Electric is the city air where angels and demons
fight
The alcoholics anonymous face their fears and cry
Lovers are locked in sweet embrace out of sight.

How was Friday are your heartaches truly hurting
Remember through that alcoholic haze you were
flirting
Excuse of the year my head was tuned but unclear
Excuse me my body reeked of wine and beer
Forgive but forget me not if you be a friend

Let us bury our indifferences this new weekend.

Green Therapy

Liberate me from mobile phones or computer zones

It is stress and strain a slow brain drain

Why I indulge in medicine for skin and bones

Try my green therapy prescribed by Doctor Sane.

Outlawed the artist Graffiti is unwelcome here

No fear no time feel nature in its prime

The towering trees flowering against summer skies

The wasps and bees and giant dragonflies

Smell babbling river water of jungle earth

And know it all evolved before your birth.

Liberate me from mobile phones or computer zones

It is stress and pains a slow brain drain

Why I indulge in medicine for worries and moans

Try my green therapy prescribed by doctor Sane.

The weeping willow tree is it crying over me

Oak trees are sculptured on grassy humped hills

Grey squirrels hop dodging sleepy daffodils

Birds sing on emerald bushes a remedy for me

Where this silver river flows presents no mystery
So be with me and sample green therapy.

Impossible You

Drowning you were gasping for breath

I threw a rope line out that was mine

Guess who nobody but death was there

Invincible and alert and far from divine

Crying you were the river masked your tears

Dying you were to trust someone impossible you.

Trapped you were in a smoky forest fire

Flames licked greedily at leafy summer trees

Surrender to this menace was your first desire

Surrender to the power the aromatic summer

breeze

Sobbing you were the fire melted those tears

Chocking you were your cries for help nobody

hears

Evoking a time where your security was impossible

you.

Lost in a lost world no sense of direction

If you are blind to there is no protection

At the school of life we attend or fear rejection

If you are of mind know that mistakes need correction

The answer is the question never solved impossible you.

New Age Poetry

Instincts

What will I from survival instinct write

Concerning life and love topics to recite

Inspire me you do on this day that's new

Always will these emotions run steadfast and true

But unexpected undetected fear startles me at night

When I do not feel alright only uptight

My inborn instincts warn me of danger

My instincts warn me of danger

So I apprehensively skate areas all round

Where there is no familiar building site

No familiar soothing city sound

People tell me there is safety in numbers

Listen and smile I'm no agile mathematician

So I must trust my primitive instincts

Instinctively a mother focuses on what baby needs

If it is time that hungry baby simply feeds

Her routine embarrasses me as at it she exceeds

She laboured not under the surgeon's knife

She was my soul mate my dear charming wife

Krysia

Her eyes are velvet green she's a super star
Her voice vibrates like an acoustic guitar
Her hair is august blonde wild and free
She's divine simply a good influence on me
She's like a lioness with a heart of gold
Sometimes her words are timid sometimes bold
She arouses undying hot fires of passion in me.

May feathered angels bow and kiss your feet
Alone my life would be shadowed or in complete
But as a lock fits a key you lock with me
Like strong roots grow up an evergreen tree
Like the sun or rain our love comes naturally
Krysia my perfumed lady my unlimited true friend
Your loving laughter is music soothing my ears
You tell me honesty must triumph in the end
You tell me deceit breeds only from our fears.

Secrets we dare not keep they niggle us when
asleep
Krysia you taught me what therapy is here for

New Age Poetry

If these head problems I create hurt me deep

I must defeat anger that furious beast of war

Krysia your love is stronger and brighter than day

Queen of mine royal I will remain for you loyal

Believe me our unique friendship is no child's play

Stay beautiful as you are driving any doubt away.

Missing

I lived as an aristocrat a proper party brat

Champers in my blood my life so tipsy, so good

The world was my lobster myself a money rat

Nobody knew I wanted normality to be understood.

Missing presumed dead or almost certainly lost

Anxiety electrifies the now unhappy incomplete

family

If there is a glimmer of hope we cope at any cost

Do you recognise this familiar photograph is it me

I was that wretched vagrant who in the city dossed

No more stiff commitments my soul sailed away

free.

Missing due to amnesia I may not quite remember

Was it on a spicy sunny day in the month of August

Or on a chilly misty day in the month of November

Call me on my mobile phone if you think you must

I will not engage you my memory lacks the thrust

Anonymous caller withheld number no contact there
No name direct the blame to that ghost society
Neglected and enigmatic we people are adrift anywhere
Unprotected against video violation I was pronounced missing.

Moonlight Melody

Night has now descended

Starlight begins glittering

All through a purple satin sky

Where people seldom watch

For full moon rises slowly overhead

Spilling light on moving water

Pulling along every single wave

Lulling dreamy wispy images

From your wonder filled eyes

Out onto this ocean with best wishes

Your mind danced thrilled

On every rippled light in sight

You've created a perfectly woven tapestry

I let think you'll surely know.

Night Fright

Daylight melts away I feel paranoia is stronger at
night
Moonlight stars glisten etched forever in dark satin
skies
From public lamp lit buildings charcoal shadows
grow or shrink
Stone city prepares itself with its surveillance
camera eyes
Mindless aliens scream abuse over what I dread to
think
Out on dreamy neon streets alcohol smitten
brawlers' brawl
Over magnetised roads motorists drive as if speed
is all.

Where do we journey as we dream there is no
music theme
A stalker followed your path so sure has motives
were unpure
Riddled with fear you froze as danger loomed near

An assault was committed almost too painful to
endure
Who knows from that memory what the aftermath
will be.

No pleasure for the prostitute whose body was her
treasure
No pleasure with out pain she's at your service
down the lane
She must earn her worth shun childbirth repent at
leisure
She must loyalty feign for her pimp or face fear
again.

No disguising this fact that any transsexual is
abstract
The unsuspecting naïve punter may not tell the tale
If he discovers from sudden shock what's under
that frock
Blinded by lust and alone he was prone to fall.

Respect

How do people compare their problems with yours?
Why do people share their talents with yours?
Key questions opened me up revelling what
personality flaws
No time for mental health professionals behind
closed doors.

At a tender age I nervously stuttered and
stammered
And the reflecting mirror mocked me constantly
It was my first, my worse ever threatening enemy
Poor self image, low esteem is what I saw
Demons of despair haunt me no longer nowhere
Faith and hope but not charity I prayed for.

Respect for the law who related whole heartedly to
it
When committing a crime did you throw a fit
If caught and convicted did you promise to quit
Crazy days were wasted home one prison cell
You started mending your old offending rebel ways

Swearing on the holy bible the truth to tell.

Respect the ambulance service, respect the fire
brigade crews
Subtract them and every day counts as bad news
Respect the funeral director, respect the church
priest
Respect the restaurant chief who served up a feast.

New Age Poetry

Schizophrenic Weather

Our orange sun rises over sea over land
Penetrating thick veils of fog and melting frost
Four seasons in one day I try to understand
The rainbow bridge was here I fear I'm lost.

Daylight cloudy skies release chilly autumn rain
This weather affects all my bittersweet moods
Ridiculous is how I act somewhat insane
Feeling of pleasure is like feeling of pain
My spirit swings up it slides down again.

Must I deliberately hibernate away at home
Or is this me courageously riding to the city
Where daylight skies are suddenly summer sunny
So seriously some people behave manic funny
I include here my self and my mental health.

No I'm untroubled by massive weight
Drifting past people as light as a feather
Wind whistling about my head not so great
I'm disgruntled now at the end of my tether

Wind howling and growling its schizophrenic
weather.

New Age Poetry

Sensitive

Windstorms and periodic rain weathering my pain

Sunshine and silver rain here we go again

Complaining if life is less than entertaining

Must I feel mad or sad or so sensitive

Cultivate the heart that knows no anger

Mediate the spirit with love let it live

Hesitate and our faith in life may blur.

You told me the truth in artistic contradiction

And chose your special way to defeat addiction

You told me the punishment never fitted the crime

You argue at reason wasting my precious time

Forgive me if I acted all so sublime

But where there is rhythm there is rhyme

Applaud my song if I gestured no mime.

Windstorms and periodic rain weathering my pain

Sunshine and silver rain here we go again

Restraining my life it proved not so entertaining

How courageous we were we scaled that mountain

John Flanagan

Shades of Insomnia

No nightmare through darkness will I willingly ride
Hide horrid secrets not me I try to confide
Do not disturb please stop your loud snoring
Dear wife told me but how she was snoring
Sleeping away my day clever it is not
Sleeping at night guards against mental rot

Why there are people live night dreaming all day
Why there are people live day dreaming all night
What's worse if we reverse the wrong way
Drug intoxication and desperation is our sad plight
Neurosis and psychosis are riotous shades of
insomnia
Sleep walking sleep talking over a shattered career.

I slept not nor ate for one month maybe two
And ended up a detainee at a human zoo
Sleep deprivation self persecution it was cruel
Now I counsel with the Wiseman not the fool.

Now I appreciate retiring to bed early not late

New Age Poetry

No family feuding which often kept me awake

No more hooting out with the owls I feel great

What else is there but prayer for heaven's sake.

Snobburbia

Transport me by speed train through this space tunnel
Over lettuce green pastel fields crooked tree shadows fell
Over the multiple arched stone bridge above the railroad
Where on observation this was it our common destination
On time were we released at the platform station.

Sniff the sunny breeze adopt those airs and graces
How you sketched disgust etched in stern women's faces
The town clown is hooked hardcore to community service
His skill you will reminisce like that first kiss
Percy the pervert photographed fresh garden flowers
No protest police issued a warrant for his arrest
Gladys's garden flowers were the envy of her friends

New Age Poetry

She was so below middle class status not rich

Her reputation that of a calculating snobby bitch

So you love fine food dine at Betty's cafeteria

Here there is an atmosphere of distasteful hysteria

You reserved no meal table with a window view

You were pampered and professed the service as

inferior

Is this all a day dream what do I know

I'm not sad but glad we departed form snobburbia.

John Flanagan

Student Scenario

Enrol eager student at university or college

One day our sunny skies will be rainy grey

One day you may graduate with carnal knowledge

One day you pray exorcise the cunning devil away

How we studied at our exams learned the scams

How we were in unison bleating like lambs.

So it was house hunting to a degree for me

It serves us right we party day or night

My grant money is not enough life is tough

A student needs time off for regular respite

Life is tainted with misery what a bitch

But my parents are influential and rich.

I was taught not to valve people's property

What a game no shame no sense of guilt

Human relationships we develop blossom and wilt

Lust was a ramble in the jungle of regret

Life is a gamble if you lose to debt.

My educated accent is aloof hide the truth

New Age Poetry

My common sense in question lacks the proof.

John Flanagan

The Happy Medium

Hello happy conclusions wherever

You think you're going

Light up look you're senses knowing

Switch on now breezes blowing

The happy medium is showing you up

No it's no use crying

No its no use denying

Yes it's happy just flying you up

Yes it takes no time at all

Yes any size, shape or hue

Variety is nothing new

Nothing that we cannot do

 The happy medium is showing you

Anything performed now what'll you do

Split a second in two

Then mend it back coloured sky blue

Anything now what'll you do

Play yourself butterfly on the summer breeze

Or wiley wasp winged insect displeased

No it's no use crying

No it's no denying

New Age Poetry

Yes it's happy just flying you up.

Sunday Complexion

A bright cheerful chrome yellow sun glared
Weightless white clouds
Moved across a brilliant blue sky
Casting pale grey shadows
Over mild green meadows and forest fields
Over high shaded opaque and umber cliffs
The shifting shadows soon disappeared
Where there strongly surged
A magnificent trichromatic ocean
Crashing incessantly upon the shingle shore
Up above gulls circled screeching
Diving down snatched up frightened fish
The gulls looked pleased, looked proud
Some now sit on rocking rolling waves
Some fly espy cheeky children happily playing
They are running face cheeks both flushed
They are walking every which way
Dogs sniffle scamper for fun
When chased by the water side
Elderly couples stroll peacefully by
Minding their own private affairs

New Age Poetry

The ocean crashes upon the wet sandy shore

Sounding like one thousand rifles fired

Against those seaweed covered rocks

Wind blew hard but couldn't equal

The tremendous volume of the sea.

The Unholy Curse

What stubborn mule madness what tearful
heartache sadness
With medication you subdue facial expressions of
distress
Brain cells dying you are tired trying to cope
But where there is a prayer there is hope
At times I struggle and address a smile
At the adult baby who is now so senile.

Tell me honestly if this was considered sacrilege
Securing those sacred house tools inside the fridge
Your bodily functions are not what they once were
Your mind like a radio programmed on past years
Memories so of this day nothing but a blur
At home you expect servile robot routine service
On your face there appears a mask of bliss.

My requests for help you seem to arrogantly ignore
Dreaming in that chair while the world hobbes by
This I know no one alive loves you more
Occasionally anxiety attacks me and how I cry

New Age Poetry

I'm your twenty four seven carer not a slave
I'm your partner guide me not to my grave.

Think

Think whose shape I exist in
Am I wearing fat or poor thin?
Do I wear a skippy smile upon a whiskered face?
Or hold a barren stubble grin out of place
Think how strong I must be
My mighty muscles get in the way of me
Think now how I'm so-so weak
Can't move my tongue from cheek to cheek
Can't raise up a whispering noise
Can't hold my breath in long period poise
Think why if I can
I'm in this human race man
And who's out raced original sin
Think whose shape I'm existing in.

New Age Poetry

Trial and Error

Girl greets toy boy coy boy greets gay uptown girl

Girl wants urgently to be boy boy wants to be girl

Behind your eyes hazy crazy dreams are born and
surprise

Are you hopelessly trapped in the wrong body
wrong size

Do you diet yourself craving for that slim trim body
prize

Are you sketching out right a future so bright and
new

Are not frosted silver night stars displayed again for
you.

Explain to me today how we get depressed and
diseased

Why that local Disney city council acted as they
pleased

Liberal animal lover's let their dogs pollute public
parks

Out of number ten for common sense they earned
no full marks

If it were not for raged motorists we would live
longer lives
Imagine how safe it could be for beloved children or
wives
But like busy bees we hustle bustle over our
homely hives.

Tell me why dogged politicians poke a finger in
every pie
The truth we hear is hard to swallow but not a
public lie
Tell me why rich beggars get richer while poor
beggars die
There is so little compassion in these fashion
worlds we cry
Catwalk queens get paraded and vanity appears all
up graded
No way is old age concealed by youthful cosmetics
yet we try
True beauty always unfaded for me wins any
contest unaided.

New Age Poetry

Explain to me if you must why justice is based on trust

Crown courts at times party for that tattooed rap clown

Who may ask to holiday in jails if punishment on him fails

There the sober jury sit in quiet fury no smile no frown

Imagine the offender lick his lips or bite them finger nails

When the judge at once spins a coin calling heads or tails

Shall that final judgement be answered by applause or wails

No point shrinking from stark terror this is all trial and error.

John Flanagan

Valentine's Message

She is the woman you so discreetly admire
She is the woman you do secretly desire
Who on earth compares to her beauty or grace
She is Venus you are Mars when face to face
She is a forest nymph ever young never old
He is attractive and lonely, fearless and bold.

He is the notorious Romeo and you his Juliet
He pledges his love without trace of regret
Who on earth compares to his compelling charm
He is cupid with bow and arrows but feel not alarm
He is cute plays the lute as any one knows
She is in ecstasy no time for worries or woes.

So be my darling Valentine I will be yours
There is no hidden message no hidden clause
Let the orchestra strike up our favourite tune
Dance with me slowly under a silver white moon
Romance with me surely this night is ours alone
Kiss me darling or my love may stay unknown.

Waiting is frustrating

Green man versus red man at the pelican crossing
Green man or red man signal which is bossing
The pedestrians and motorists feel it humiliating
At the city signed bus stop I was waiting
That corporation bus never seemed to arrive
My destination the doctors waiting room how
nauseating
If apathy attacks me how will I survive
Waiting is intimidating and I cursed authority.

Waiting officially you robbed the robber
Waiting innocently you abused the abuser
Waiting dramatically to hunt the hunter
Waiting expectantly to love the lover
Illustrating my rapture at the presence of her.

Winter was dreary we were weary of stormy skies
Waiting how frustrating but tomorrow never dies
Anticipating sexy summer when our spirits dance
And romance not the reverse we try to enhance.

We Are Cars

Ignition on hand brake released I slip into gear
No stopping me now I'm pulling out anyhow
Check in my mirror that nobody is near
Off I drive personal safety my first vow
We are cars we are shooting stars.

Cruising above the road I resemble a nodding doll
Squinting at the sun so my eyes I must shade
Car pressure gauge tells its time for petrol
At the hospital station elation my transfusion paid
We are shooting stars we are cars.

My car wheels are spinning through the silver rain
My one notion is that we are poetry in motion
This is me signalling on your traffic light lane
We are cars we are shooting stars.

At night in this metal shelled car I feel secure
At night I drive where moon Shadowed buildings
are
What vice is in store I ignore the law

At daylight nothing to report it was only sport

We are shooting stars we are cars.

LaVergne, TN USA
03 February 2010
172019LV00001B/22/P